FOREVER I DO

Successfully Journeying Through the First Years of Marriage

For the committed, engaged, newlywed and experienced couple desiring a fresh perspective

Donette P. Williamson, M.S.

Cover Design: Pastor Roderick Rolle

ISBN: 978-976-95666-0-6
January 2014
Webpage: **www.donettewilliamson.com**
Email address: donettewilliamson1977@gmail.com

Disclaimer

All material in this book is intended for informational and
educational purposes only. Any use or application of the
contents of this book is at the reader's discretion and at the
reader's sole responsibility.

Readership Reviews

The book was a very interesting and inspiring read. It had a realness to it that prompted comparisons to our own lives. An amazing feature showcasing this was the couple's discussions at the end of each chapter. Conversations were had due to these discussions that forced us to go deeper than the surface and brought to light notable differences and similarities.
Dwan Archer & Cynette Micklewhite, engaged 5 months.

This book is truly amazing! We both related to your principles. It is an excellent guide in realizing that as a married couple things are not so black and white as there was no guide handed out at the wedding as to how to get it right. It gives a new couple like us hope and optimism that we can do this!
Reuben & Deschanel Hamilton, married 1 year.

You have certainly given a "fly on the wall" experience of your marriage. The principles clearly outlined in this book has been "de-fluffed" and "de-sugarcoated". Thank you for liberally sharing with us the key ingredients and recipe to your vibrant marriage.
Larry and Terah Bowe, happily married 7 years.

These principles would make great discussions in a marriage club meeting or single ministry. Easy reading, deep, great questions. This book has given me more food for thought.
Prescola Pinder, married 30 years.

The author dared to be open and vulnerable, people appreciate that! This inspired me to rekindle some things in my marriage and could help many people! It had good humour and the author has great writing ability!
Ephraim Forbes, married 30 years.

TABLE OF CONTENTS

Acknowledgements

There are so many persons that inspired this book. I wish to begin with my loving husband Giles, who in his comical way told me to get over my rant about relationship and marital issues and use my creativity and insights to write a book. I thank him for his support and for allowing me to share our story with our reading audience. It is hoped that by reading Forever I Do, couples worldwide can be inspired to live successful and prosperous married lives, one day at a time using simple and practical principles that kept us going throughout our formative years of marriage.

I further wish to thank my mother, aunts, step-mom, in-laws, friends and extended family members who have encouraged me to pursue my talents. Their direct and indirect efforts in assisting me to achieve this milestone will never be forgotten.

Special mention to my editors and proofreaders, Antoinette Lewis-Deveaux, Ephraim Forbes, Prescola Pinder, Shelly Archer, Nadia Cash and Nikita Moss-Woodside. Also much thanks to my book cover designer Pastor Roderick Rolle. Your invaluable contributions of editing insights, constructive criticism, time, creativity and willingness to see me succeed are appreciated beyond words.

I finally wish to give thanks to God, my inspiration for granting me wisdom and insight to pursue this endeavour.

Foreword

Cicero said that "the first bond of society is marriage". Indeed it the wellspring for all other institutions. Yet its importance to society has been trivialized and casualized like none other. In most cases there is no preparation for this most critical estate even though some of the deepest struggles of life will occur in this most primary relationship affected by The Fall. This is why this volume of ten principles gives me hope. The reader is challenged to take an introspective look at one's personal life and marriage life.

With the zest of a seasoned counsellor, the author shares content beyond her years of marital experience. With simplicity, clarity and yet with depth, this volume catapults the reader to a reality show which bares the soul of a continuing and successful marital journey.

The reader is taken on a tour of a living museum that is under construction with a foundation that can withstand the inevitability of life's storms. This volume is packed with insightful, purposeful, directional, meaningful and practical information. I

love its "homey" feel that makes one want to read more as the author has skillfully avoided ivory tower ideas and pious evasions. From Building Bonds of Unity and Continue to Date to Establishing Effective

Communication, Creating Your Own Paradise and "Ourness", the author tackles the uncomplicated areas that can cause the deepest hurts from the one closest to you.

I am also particularly pleased that the author helps the reader with guided reflections so that the content is cemented in the mind and there are handles to clutch. Indeed the ten principles expounded show us the beauty of balance as the marital journey is simplified and de-cluttered. The author's openness and vulnerability draws us to a vivid transparency. Indeed if anyone has been derailed, this volume has enough "umph" to get anyone back on track. If you want to stay on track, then these pages are for you.

God created marriage and designed it with a specific purpose and plan. But ignoring his design will lead to chaos, confusion, pain and suffering. Drink the content of this volume and you will be taking a prescription that works in any culture and will assist you to avoid the quagmire of the unnecessary and you will live skillfully. I recommend this book to all, but especially to those who have the gift of marriage and are looking forward to enjoying and reflecting the image of God.

Dr. Deanza Cunningham
Senior Pastor
Christ Community Church
Nassau, Bahamas

Preface

I wrote "Forever I Do" as a guide, to give insight into how my husband and I successfully journeyed through our first five years of marriage. We still love each other and want to continue this wonderful journey together. This call came out of the growing trend of failed marriages in my local community and the multiplicity of misconceptions and perceptions of marriage held by so many.

In 2007 when we married, we personally knew five other couples who married within that same year. Unfortunately by 2012, there was one divorce and two of the couples suffer from tremendous challenges ranging from alcoholism to pedophilia. Therefore, this reality led me to ponder why it is that we are enjoying a good marriage thus far and so many others are experiencing tremendous challenges keeping their marriages in tact.

For some reason my thoughts initially garnered around external influences and I thought about how, in my opinion, Hollywood, i.e. soap operas, movies, prime time television and its promoters have been very successful in trivializing the true beauty and sanctity of marriage. We become happy when the vixen's husband cheats on her, or the nice hardworking gardener gets the unscrupulous millionaire's wife. Somehow we rationalize those types of acts with the "payback's-a-you-know-what" mentality. However, if the show lasts as long as the soap operas do, we see that the unending circle of deception, lies and hurt superimpose over the goodwill and nature of the characters and the wheel of misfortune never seems to stop spinning.

I, however, don't wish to posture that everything about Hollywood is inherently bad but the reality is that it can and in some cases does affect our cognition if we do not actively try to filter out the negative aspects. As parents, my husband and I find ourselves singing those repetitive toddler cartoon songs our toddler is exposed to on a daily basis. This caused me to question whether repeated exposure to events that make light of marital relationships can influence our thought processes and behaviors. Is it possible that we too can begin to accept these behaviors as being the norm and standard for family life and marriage? The truth is it takes work and a determined mindset to survive the many tests your marriage will experience.

Many of you reading this book are probably saying "Yup I have that determined ability to make my marriage work! Or would you question my audacity to suggest otherwise?" You perhaps may be thinking "*Of course I expect my marriage to work, to have longevity, to spend the rest of my life with the love of my life!*" Ah, but the proof is in the pudding. Look around you, in your families, work places, civic organizations and even religious institutions. Are couples in your spheres of influence trending upward or downward in their marriages? Are they generally happy and fulfilled or stressed and challenged in their marriages?

Now I want you to take a few minutes to focus on all the married couples you know, whether they are young, middle aged, older, religious or non-religious. How many of them do you honestly want your marriage to emulate? If you could be a "fly on the wall," whose bedroom wall or kitchen window sill would you like to land on? What does that couple practice or believe in that set them apart from others? What gives them the impetus to be genuinely contented with each others' company in the midst of their marital challenges and strive toward enjoying a lifetime together? Well, the odds are if there are 10 different couples you can identify, there will likely be over 10 different answers, remedies and advice you will get as to how to make your marriage work. However, if you dissect all these viewpoints, I believe they can be characterized into certain principles.

When I refer to a principle, I am describing a mutually agreed upon system of beliefs or behaviors. They act as a foundation for how couples respond to each other when challenging situations test their marriages. How they act, react and govern themselves.

On the morning of the birth of this book, several questions surfaced in my mind. I questioned why marriages in general are so complex. I questioned why hubby and I were so content and had such a genuinely loving relationship and great friendship. Then my thoughts shifted to some of the dysfunctional marriages in our spheres of influence. My frustration brewed, which led me to channel it into penning seven principles that came to my mind immediately that we unconsciously are guided by and live by. Due to discussions through my initial editing process, three other principles evolved and were added to my original list.

I will use these few pages to share our experiences. It is my hope that you see the value in these principles and guidelines and feel free to tailor them to your relationship and marriage. It is our desire for you to reap the success that my husband and I have experienced thus far. Your application of these ten principles will be as easy or as difficult as each of you make it. It will only work if you both give it equal effort and commitment. I would suggest that before you continue reading that you answer the questions in the Personal Assessment page to gauge your present personal belief system. Subsequent to each principle provided, you and your spouse, fiancée or significant other will be asked to openly and honestly assess yourselves individually and as a unit. It is my desire that this time together will either shape or reshape the present course of your relationship to a positive and upward trend toward success and viability.

PERSONAL ASSESSMENT

1. Why am I here on earth? i.e. What do I believe my purpose for being born is?

2. What do I want to accomplish in my lifetime?

3. What do I want to accomplish in my marriage?

4. How do I respond to the world i.e. family, friends, colleagues when I am:

    - ❖ Happy?
    - ❖ Sad?
    - ❖ Disappointed?
    - ❖ Frustrated?
    - ❖ Angry?

5. How do I respond my spouse, fiancée or significant other when I am:

    - ❖ Happy?
    - ❖ Sad?
    - ❖ Disappointed?
    - ❖ Frustrated?
    - ❖ Angry?

6. How is my spouse, fiancée, or significant other affected when I am:

    - ❖ Happy?
    - ❖ Sad?
    - ❖ Disappointed?
    - ❖ Frustrated?
    - ❖ Angry?

7. Where do I see myself as a husband/wife/parent:

- ❖ 1 year from now?
- ❖ 5 years from now?
- ❖ 10 years from now?
- ❖ 25 years from now?

How We Met

My husband and I met in December of 2005 after a close female friend of his, took part in a match making ploy. This ploy ended with her threatening me that she would continue to harass me by calling every half hour until I called him to make a date. Folks, it was not an idle threat as I began to test it, after her second or third call, I decided to get her off my back and give him a call.

Before I delve into the first discussion, I must state that at the age of 28, I was resigned to living a happy single life, if that was my destiny. I had already gone through the pity partying sessions with myself, the self-blame game of being too ugly, boring and all that nonsense. These sessions had evolved into an epiphany of self-contentment, self-worth and wholeness. At that time, I wasn't looking for a boyfriend so it was with great hesitation that I called him.

My recollection of the ensuing chain of events is that the first call was pleasant and engaging. I honestly, can't remember what we talked about, but I do remember we could not decide on a day to meet, as it was the Christmas holiday season and every day thereafter either of us had some kind of obligation. I suggested we wait until the New Year to set a date, but my husband to be insisted that we had to meet before the year ended. We decided on the 29th of December. The chosen venue was Marina Village at Atlantis,

Nassau, Bahamas. It was a hot spot at the time and I deemed it safe, as it was a popular tourist and local venue.

Hubby, as I will affectionately refer to him throughout this book, in my ignorance suggested that I park at a time share lodge in the same vicinity of the hotel we agreed to meet. I was unaware that his family had a gift shop there, and he would be in a position to get the first full view of my appearance, possibly to bail out if I didn't fit the bill. The date was very engaging and cordial and it lasted pass 12:00 a.m. the next morning. We found ourselves talking the night away about everything and nothing, genuinely enjoying each others' company.

Initially, before the date began, my thoughts consisted of just needing to get this date over with so I can get his friend off of my back My impression afterward, was that he was a really nice guy, not my typical dream date but he was definitely worth another date. The next day, my close family friend, who was also mutual friends with hubby's friend called and told me what hubby's account of the date was. I can't remember all the details, but I do recall her being able to describe what I wore from head to toe. Hubby denies being so detailed, so I guess the mysterious "fly on the wall" shared that information with my friend. Two years later, we made that monumental step and got married and have been pressing our way forward on this wonderful journey ever since.

PRINCIPLE #1

~

Building Bonds of Unity

During my outlining stage of these writings the first and most important principle I thought of was Unity. I'm not trying to be condescending in any way, because you may be thinking "Isn't it obvious that we're unified because we've taken the biggest, most important step together? Joining your life with someone else forever, my friend, it's just the tip of the iceberg and you'll soon see why.

Unity in my humble opinion is the core component required for a successful marriage. This involves each individual coming together and being on one accord. In the Christianity religion, typical weddings require couples to respond to their vows with the phrase "I do." I have also witnessed wedding ceremonies whereby a sand or salt covenant was used.

This covenant involved the use of three clear vessels, one that was held by the bride and the other by the groom and the third and larger vessel was used as the primary vessel. The bride and groom were asked to simultaneously pour their salt or sand content into the larger vessel. The meaning behind that act signified the union of each other's beliefs and total lives. The idea also suggests that just as the bride and groom's sand content merged and was intertwined together, neither of them can decipher whose sand is whose. This is how their marriage life is to be mirrored. The main sand vessel represents the couples merging of their goals, their vision for their immediate family unit, their child rearing practices, their financial goals, their families, their hearts, dreams and lives together. It goes without saying that everyone still has his or her own identity, that quality is innate. However, when it comes to an issue, person or decision that affects the marriage they must present a united front and put all individual ideals on the side for the betterment of the marriage and family unit. For hubby and me, we realized that there were three core areas that we both shared and were unified in. These were: our spiritual belief system, our emotions and understanding of each other's emotions and our life goals as individuals and as a couple.

Spiritual Unity

Our spiritual unity signifies our sharing of similar values of the basic things we believe in. For example, the equality of men and women in life and in marriage. It means that our marriage is a union between the two of us and not anyone else. It means that if we disagree on an issue, we should discuss it to gain an understanding of each other's views and be empathetic toward those views. It means that our marriage is a priority above all other people and things, and it means that we both believe in God. By the time we decided to get married we had a good sense of what each other's spiritual stances were. We prayed and read books about dating and preparing for marriage, we completed workbooks and we attended relationship conferences. We did anything to help us grow and create opportunities to share and discuss our worldviews and beliefs. We believe in the male being accountable as the head in marriage, but that both husband and wife were equal partners in the relationship and in making decisions.

I once heard the comment that people who are praying together can't fight. I thought there was some merit to it because, for us, prayer forces us to rise up to a deeper level of ourselves because we believe that we are ultimately accountable to a higher power in our lives that is, God. Therefore, when we pray we are saying that we manage our lives but we know that a higher power is at work on our behalf and we must seek the greater good for ourselves, and let go of all selfish motives to achieve that greater good. For persons who may not be religious, spiritual unity for you may require you to discuss and write down what you believe in personally and how those beliefs can translate into how you live your lives as a couple and raise your children. There must be a general consensus that you can draw from when having to make decisions that affect your lives. Without it you may possibly find yourselves at constant forks in the road as you make decisions based on your moral and ethical belief systems.

Emotional Unity

Emotional unity entails both hubby and I having a understanding of and appreciation for each other's mood and how to react or not react to each other's actions, feelings and thoughts. It means that hubby knows if he doesn't look at me whenever I am talking about a serious matter I would feel disrespected. Therefore, he has to turn down the sound on the television, or stop surfing the internet. It means that if hubby raises his voice during a discussion, it signals to me that he is frustrated over an issue which may not even be related to me and he needs to vent or go into his man cave. I must let him exhale and not be a nag even though I feel the need to resolve the issue immediately. Emotional unity calls for the protection of one spouse's emotions during those times when they are most vulnerable and to do what you can to bring him or her back to that "happy place" or normal emotional functioning.

I grew up in a single parent family with my mother but spent most weekends with my dad and his family. My hubby on the other hand grew up in a nuclear family setting. Even though I was often exposed to married life through my dad and step-mom, much of my influence came through my mother. I learned from her to be strong, a survivor, a hard-worker, determined, to sacrifice and to save from her. I learned that I didn't need a man to take care of me and I was fully capable of taking care of myself. I also decided that I wanted a nuclear family because rearing a child by oneself was very burdensome and called for much sacrifice and self-denial. My hubby however, lived a more financially comfortable life as both of his parents had better jobs and better pay than my mother did.

Therefore many of the struggles and sacrifices I experienced he did not experience. My mom couldn't afford name brand clothing or shoes but his parents could. She had to save those monies for my private school education. I didn't get new school uniforms every year. I wore the same uniform throughout elementary school. When I graduated to high school I got new uniforms and wore them until I was elected prefect in the twelfth grade and had to change uniforms. My husband got new uniforms and name brand shoes at the beginning of every new school year.

I gave this brief synopsis to paint a picture of how our lives differed and therefore shaped our emotional experiences toward life and relationships differently. For me, I was more guarded of men since my dad married another woman who I have grown to love dearly. I didn't trust that a man could just give a gift without wanting anything in return. I had to stay on top of the game at all times. Therefore, initially during dating, hubby's frequent purchases of gifts or his willingness to be the first to make amends when we had an argument was difficult for me to trust emotionally. Perhaps it was his high emotional security and sensitivity from being in a balanced nuclear family that caused my hubby to be sensitive to my guarded and harsh exterior. However, he took the time to study me and figure out what made me tick, upset, happy and he accommodated it. I suppose, like most men in my sphere of influence, he wasn't that hard to figure out. Life was either black or white for my hubby, he either liked or disliked something, so the emotional test of hubby wasn't as wasn't as challenging for me. We both had to learn to trust each other with our most deepest feelings and failures and hoped that the other would be accepting and forgiving. This is why it is so important in one's dating relationship to be transparent and not hide one's feelings whether happy, sad, frustrated or angry. How will your spouse know how to react if he or she is not exposed to them until post-wedding? We realized that in order to be our "best selves" we had to be emotionally stable, so we resolved that we would partner in ensuring that we contributed positively to that end. This includes simple things such as hubby keeping the bathroom door closed so that I don't feel the air-conditioning chill when coming out of the shower, to putting away the lap top he bought me so our toddler wouldn't play with it. It's little things that usually cause arguments and dissent and if they are not resolved they can metastasize like a cancerous tumor. Therefore, we seek to minimize situations that will cause unnecessary emotional dissent toward one another.

Unity in your Life Goals

Unity in your Life Goals is indicative of the things you both want to achieve in life as a couple. It involves not dismissing your personal endeavors, but defining how you can merge your individual goals to enhance and accentuate your destiny as a couple. I consider myself a big dreamer. While hubby and I dated, I began a business plan for farming and other entrepeneurial ventures. His profession is in Information Technology, but he also enjoyed the business aspect of his work due to experience with managing roles his parents' businesses. He didn't seek to hamper or discourage my dreams, but would lend his business insight as to how to enhance my business ideas and bring them more technologically in line with modern standards and practices. If I came up with an idea he didn't agree with, instead of dismissing it out rightly, he would come up with a twist or a way we could modify it to be more appealing or feasible.

Hubby and I believed that whoever had the strength in a particular area would spearhead that project, whether it was finances, dinner choices or organizing an event. We both wanted to own our own home and not rent for a long time. My mom blessed us with a property as our wedding gift. Therefore, we gave ourselves a two year time line to be in our home and saved and sacrificed to achieve that goal. I was deemed the CEO of the initial phase of our building project. I utilized my strengths as a great organizer and manager. I made all of the contacts, calls and appointments and hubby would show up for the appointments and we would discuss the options. This was such an special and exciting time for us. I learned about the good taste he has as a male and discovered how knowledgeable he is about technical things such as plumbing, building plans etc.

During the construction phase of our building project, I took the back seat. He was the one who visited the site everyday and brought the pictures to include me as a part of the construction phase. When it was time to put in the closets, to choose the paint and to decorate, my attitude was "call me." Therefore early in our relationship, hubby and I recognized and maximized on each other's strengths. Mine, being the business and organizational expertise and his being more of a technical expertise. We learned things about each other we probably would not have known that aided in allowing the other to take the backseat without feeling left out of a project. Because we understood our strengths and knew that letting the stronger person take charge of a venture would be beneficial to the success of that venture we undertook, plans went along relatively smoothly.

For some of you, as parents in a marriage, unity may suggest standing a united front on a decision for the children even if personally you think another option would be better. Air out your differences privately but communicate your decision as a unit to the children. Send the message to your children that whether mom (step-mom) or dad (step-dad) makes a decision, they are only wasting their time going to the next parent for a different verdict. It may require identifying who is the point person in a particular situation. For example, with everyday parenting decisions such as deciding what your children wear, eat or what social events they are allowed to attend etc., since mothers are usually the primary care-givers in the home, the children could be made to understand to come to mom for permission for those kind of decisions. In the event she isn't home, then dad would use his good judgment.

Hubby and I shared simple life goals, which were nurturing a healthy, happy family life, building our home, having children, traveling and engaging in business ventures. Virtually, using the basic measures our parents practiced for years and realizing that life didn't turn out half bad for them. I know it's not very exciting, but we believe since we had "**done us**" in our single lives such as going abroad to college, travelling, partying, socializing, there wasn't much else new to experience. But you see that's just it. Often people have grandiose ideals as to what a marriage should be, a life filled with so many great escapades, at least that's what the television shows often portrays, and some people blindly set their bars to this ever evolving standard of living. If either of us want to go bungee-jumping or sky-diving or participate in some other thrill-seeking act or wish to travel to the seven continents of the world, we still have the opportunity to do so. We just have to plan and agree on these events mutually and weigh the costs, benefits, or loss to our family life.

Our second but most important life goal was parenthood. We decided that we didn't want more than two or three children. About a year and half after moving in our home, our precious Ava came along and this was such an exciting time in our lives. We decided the time of year we wanted her to be born for school admission purposes and adjusted our family planning methods to accommodate that. However, life in its true form doesn't always evolve as smoothly as we plan. Our first pregnancy resulted into a miscarriage forcing us to confront our hurt, disappointment and self-blame over what may have caused the event. We decided that this experience would draw us closer together and not apart as hubby so delicately helped me walk through this season of grief. Seven months later Ava Marie graced our lives and we decided that hubby would be a very active part of this new journey. He was summoned to attend our doctor's visits. Of course he would make comments such as "I'm the only male in the office, something has to be wrong with that," but that only went through one of my ears and came out of the next. I knew he enjoyed hearing Ava's heartbeat and her sonograms more than I did. He was so excited, more than I was initially as I was still guarded due to having a miscarriage prior to this pregnancy. This is another emotion we worked out together by talking and as the pregnancy progressed and the movements began, I fell in love with her.

As I write this, we are currently in Ava's preschool phase and we take life as it comes. We plan projects, for the home and yard, decide on vacation plans and dream or daydream about business venture options.

Our perspective is life is short so we live day to day, enjoying every precious moment. We do this this even more so after experiencing young family members of ours die and leave minor children and relatively young couples being left single due to terminal cancer. We listened to so many horror stories of dysfunctional married couples on such a regular basis, and determined that we are blessed and chose to be grateful for this simple but rich life we were afforded. With unity as the lifeblood of our relationship we resolved that if we couldn't make a decision together then we would put it on hold until we could reach a consensus.

COUPLE DISCUSSION AND APPLICATION SECTION:

Take out a notepad and write out your responses, then discuss openly and honestly with your spouse, fiancée or significant other.

1. What is my spiritual belief system and why did I chose it? e.g. Christian, Buddhist Atheist.

2. Does my individual spiritual belief system affect our relationship positively, negatively or at all?

3. How will our spiritual belief system affect our children:-

    a) How we teach them (spiritually, morally, socially etc.)
    b) How we discipline them

4. What role do you play in ensuring your spouse, fiancée or significant other feels emotionally secure in your relationship?

5. What practical things can you do to create an environment of emotional unity in your relationship? i.e. to keep each other in his/her happy place

6. What are your life goals and does your spouse support them?

7. What are your marital goals and how will you go about achieving them?

8. What strengths do you bring into the relationship that unite you as a couple?

9. What weaknesses do you bring into the relationship that divide you as a couple?

10. How can we maximize our strengths and minimize our weaknesses to benefit each other:

    a) Personally
    b) As a family unit

11. What things can we do that can make our relationship more unified?

If your responses are diametrically opposed to each other, discuss how you can merge your ideas to benefit your marriage so that everyone feels his or her views are valued.

PRINCIPLE #2

~

Leave and Cleave

In principle number one I discussed different aspects of unity and how it is the core component of a successful married life. This now brings me to the purpose of writing principle number two and titling it "Leave and Cleave."

Leave and Cleave is the biblical principle of forsaking father and mother and solely clinging to the one you're married to. In other words, putting all persons and activities second to one's spouse. It suggests that you are now one and your spouse's concerns, wishes and well-being far supersedes that of children, parents, siblings, friends, jobs and social interests. What is so ironic is so many people want to leave but only a few want to cleave. Understand, that leave and cleave demands that you commit to a lifetime of sharing the joy, laughter, tears, hurts, pains, you name it. Whatever comes with the package that's what you both agree to share in together.

From my observations many marital problems stem from a spouse being unable to prioritize between spouse, loved ones, friends and profession. I am in no way advocating that once married you forsake socializing with or assisting family and friends. However, your spouse should always be given priority over any other person or event in your life. Your family and friends should be made to respect your time, home, marriage decisions and spouse. This premise should have been put in motion from the engagement time where boundaries were being set with regards to decisions being made by the couple regarding wedding plans regardless of the opinions of family and friends.

When a couple is dating, there are usually clear indications of the priority given to the relationship by each individual. Did mom call two or three times during your dates and you had to alter your plans to accommodate hers? Were friends over at the house almost every time you came by to visit and didn't leave shortly after you arrived at least half of the time? Did your dates get canceled to accommodate a friend's car breaking down or were you invited to tag along to assist that friend? Your spouses' responses during your dating life to these kinds of scenarios give some insight as to whether or not you would face some boundary challenges in your marriage. Conflict in the marriage may arise if you and your spouse did not set clear parameters for where you both stand during your dating relationship.

Early in our marriage, we lived a few corners away from hubby's parents. I recall many months of my hubby stopping by his parents on Sundays and coming home with a plate of food. I was often offended by this. Now, before you start judging me for being petty you must understand that I was a new wife trying to establish my "first place" status in my hubby's life. I prided myself on getting up early on Sunday mornings to cook a wholesome meal for my husband and I enjoyed doing it. So I took it as an insult that he would stop elsewhere to eat, even if at his parents' house. After a few weeks of disgruntlement I decided to voice my concerns, letting him know how this was offensive to me especially knowing that I had already cooked. Since the talk, I noticed that when asked if he wanted food from his mom, gradually hubby would respond "*my wife cooked, we have food at home.*" Yes he may have still taken a piece of meat on the go but it sent a clear message to me that he respected my efforts and feelings. I'm sure this was a big step for him as well. Let me stick a pin right here and clarify that my in-laws and I have a wonderful, loving and amicable relationship. Hubby and I welcome any invitation to dine and fellowship with them but during the formative period of our marriage we needed to solidify our new allegiances.

Making these kinds of adjustments early in our marriage was made easier as this principle was introduced to our family and friends at our wedding by our officiator during our wedding celebration. Our officiator asked our families to stand and make a public declaration to the congregation stating and I quote "I vow to stay out of their business unless asked for advice." It was comical at the time but also a serious declaration. To date, all in sundry have complied and I think that has made the transition so much smoother for us. So folks, my advice to you if you haven't already done this, set this principle in motion. Resolve to make each other a priority over parents, siblings and even children. If they didn't sign the papers with you, their opinions should have very little value in your decisions and in your way of life unless solicited by you both. It should be that you *both* mutually grant family or friends permission to impose on your marital affairs or that their opinions and advice not be asked at all. However, it is strongly advised that you both identify an experienced couple or a married friend who you both trust, respect and mutually agree on to consult with. Refer to this person or persons whenever you both come to a fork in the road whereby external assistance and objectivity would bring more clarity to your issue and be helpful to resolving conflict. The key is **mutual agreement** whether a marriage counselor, religious counsellor, friend or family member. Wait until you both are in an amicable place to discuss with each other who your point person(s) are and who you both would feel comfortable letting into your marriage, for the sole purpose of moving the relationship forward in a spirit of objectivity and resolution.

COUPLE DISCUSSION AND APPLICATION SECTION:

Take out a notepad and write out your responses, then discuss openly and honestly with your spouse, fiancée or significant other.

1. List in order of priority the following and explain why each is important to you?

   ❖ Spouse
   ❖ Children
   ❖ Parents
   ❖ Siblings
   ❖ Friends
   ❖ Jobs
   ❖ Civic/social/religious affiliations

2. Has your spouse ever expressed concern over feeling second class to another entity in your life? If so, how can you avoid future occurrences?

3. How do you feel whenever your spouse seems to attend to someone else's needs before yours?

4. What specific things can you do to demonstrate that your spouse is number one in your life?

5. Identify a person or persons you feel comfortable sharing a problem with. Discuss whether or not your spouse would be comfortable with you having this person as a confidante whenever you (individually or as a couple) need an opinion/insight about a marital issue or concern.

PRINCIPLE #3

~

Develop a Devotional Life Together

What is your core value system personally? How can you merge it to become **"Our"** core values system? What matters most to you as a couple? What do you truly believe in? In my opinion, one's core value system is what is left after the views of parents, family, friends, your community and the wider world have been filtered out. It is that basic belief and thought system that is truly what you govern your life and relationship by.

Granted these answers should be concrete before you walk the aisle but if you're already married, it suggests that there are some basic things that you both agree on and want to achieve in life. I understand that many of you who are reading this book may be of differing religions or not religious at all. However, it is vital to your relationship to set time to commune together. For hubby and me, it is praying. We pray for ourselves, our marriage, Ava, our families, colleagues or others who may have needs that are beyond our physical ability to provide for. We share concerns about life and our communities and insights from God, ideas, dreams and future aspirations.

Developing a devotional life together, causes us to stay connected on a level that is deeper than ourselves. We rejoice whenever we see our prayers answered. For example, when we prayed for a couple who struggled with a miscarriage and the difficulties of getting pregnant, who, one year and a half later, invited us to attend their son and daughter's christening. Another example is when I didn't succeed in getting pregnant after six months of attempts post miscarriage, deciding to pray, getting pregnant a month later. Or perhaps, us sharing in the disappointment of unanswered prayers for the healing of our loved ones who died. Being saddened, but encouraged to appreciate the blessing of the time they spent with us and for our lives being spared thus far. Even if you're not religious, read a book or mutually enjoyable literature and then set time to discuss it and find the greater meaning behind this wonderful gift of life given to you daily. Perhaps there is a relaxing recreational activity that you enjoy as a couple such as hiking, kayaking or cycling. Use this time to discuss those profound things in life to get a sense of where your spouse is spiritually and emotionally. Maybe you can use this time to share that crazy idea or dream you had but have not quite crystallized in your mind. You may be surprised to learn how supportive and innovative you can become as a team.

A common phrase I hear and often repeat is "great minds think alike." The fact that you decided to make a lifelong commitment suggests there are qualities that drew you to this person. You can be instrumental in birthing the greatness that lies within your spouse that hasn't been realized as yet. How will you ever know if you don't come together and get a concrete sense of your thoughts, ideas and dreams? A devotional time can appeal to this higher dimension of marital communion for you and your spouse.

COUPLE DISCUSSION AND APPLICATION SECTION:

Take out a notepad and write out your responses, then discuss openly and honestly with your spouse, fiancée or significant other.

1. What recreational things do I/can I do to relax?

2. When do I take time to meditate on my life, marriage, job or family?

3. Would I feel comfortable sharing aspects of my meditation with my spouse, fiancée or significant other? If not, why not?

4. What things do my spouse, fiancée or significant other enjoy doing in his or her spare time to relax and meditate that I feel comfortable sharing in?

5. How can we merge our recreational activities to stay in touch with our belief systems and personal goals in life and as a couple?

After you have found a forum to connect with on a spiritual level, specify a day and time you will come together on a regular basis to grow this element of your relationship.

PRINCIPLE #4

~

Establish Effective Communication

I've heard this phrase or some semblance of it more than once "Talk through your problems, don't bottle them or you will burst." As a School Psychologist, I understand the philosophy behind those sentiments. Nonetheless, when I think about the term communication, I envision a broader meaning than just the exchange of information. Communication, in its entirety, encompasses how we transmit messages, information, feelings, views, facts and thoughts verbally and non-verbally.

In a marriage, non-verbal communication is often as equally as effective in conveying messages as verbal communication. For example, the message of dissent can be conveyed by the jerking of the shoulder when being touched gently or by displaying signs of frustration with rolled eyes, slammed doors or pots when cooking, or a grunt or throat clearing for disapproval. Nonverbal communication can also convey warm sentiments with a light kiss on the forehead, replacing of the sheets over a cold body through the night or a hand being held during the sharing of bad or good news.

I didn't initially outline communication as a principle, primarily because it came so naturally to hubby and me. However, after a second thought, I had to include it due to it being a staple and pillar in our relationship. Also, it would have been remiss of me not to include it for the many couples who may struggle with communication.

It must be understood that communication is so much deeper than just the spoken word and it is integral to relationship survival. There are deaf couples who have remained married. Therefore, being able to audibly speak is obviously not the main criteria for effective communication. Hubby and I realized that the *soul of communication* is just that "the spirit behind how and why we say or do, what we say or do." My mom would often say "it's not what you say, but how you say it" Words can hurt or heal, and hubby and I learned that we both carry an arsenal of hurtful weapons of marriage destruction in our words. However, we had to learn to discipline ourselves to use our words constructively towards one another even when angry. This suggested that we had to at times step back and temper our words or come back at a later time when our anger levels decreased a few notches before stating how we felt.

This was a hard lesson learnt over time for the both of us and is still a work in progress for me. I've heard during the course of a lifetime that women speak more than 50 percent more than men do a day. Females are natural communicators even as infants. I tested this hypothesis when my colleague and I compared our female and male toddlers who are less than a month apart. My Ava's language development is much more advanced than her son's. She also shared that when her older daughter was a toddler at the same age of our children, she too was more advanced verbally than her son is presently. So ladies let's give ourselves the edge on this principle. Therefore, with this premise in mind it is highly likely that females verbally communicate more than males and are therefore, more likely to use "weapons of marriage destruction" more often than their male counterparts. Therefore, as females in relationships, we must constantly work on tempering our words.

As aforementioned, communication goes far beyond just mere words, but how you use those words to convey information, to empower or to break down. At my lingerie shower, I got little messages of advice from all of the attendees. One of my very good married friend's advice to me was to temper my tongue. I laughed then but now cherish the wisdom behind that advice. My bold personality comes with a swift and sharp tongue at times I admit. There are very few people I back down from expressing my opinions to and that's often due to respect or not wanting to go through the hassle of a back and forth altercation.

To give you a sense of our communication styles anyone who knows me well would describe me as being a straight talker, open and opinionated person. My husband is more relaxed, non controversial and easy going. We are both talkative but he has to be in a more relaxed environment to speak freely, whereas I usually feel comfortable communicating in most environments. He, therefore, had to work through my strong will and mindset of being in control, barriers of being hurt from past relationships and independence from growing up in a single parent home with a strong willed mother. During our courtship, if he paid for dinner on one date, I would rush to pay for the next dinner date. I couldn't allow him to think he was taking care of me. He would often buy me flowers, and though it was such a pleasure receiving them in the office, initially, I had my guard up wondering what his motives were. When I had my crazy tantrums when I was upset with him, he would calmly respond and make contact with me even if I hung up on him. I thought this was unbelievable! Perhaps, being an alpha male, hubby found taking me on a challenge of "taming the shrew".

So by the time we were engaged he knew all sides of me the good, bad and the ugly. I was myself ladies, I bore it all, if he did or said something I didn't like, I told him. He was also very open and frank about his past "sins" baring all risks of my "goody two shoes self" to leave him. We discovered what the proverbial questions were when we communicated with each other. They were firstly, "What message do we want to send intentionally? Secondly, What messages do we send unconsciously or unintentionally to each other?" Hubby sending flowers to me for no special occasion, conveyed the message, "You're in my heart and I want to see you smile." I know this because he would call my colleague to find out my response or he would call me when he thought the bouquet arrived to gauge my response. With the help of Gary Chapman's book "The Five Love Languages" we began to understand how we communicate our love to one another. Hubby's primary love languages are giving gifts, acts of service and words of affirmation. My primary love languages are spending quality time and acts of service. Therefore, hubby buying me gifts during our courtship or his taking Ava and me for a Sunday drive for ice cream is his expression of love. My cooking for him or helping him with his coursework during his college days or writing or proofreading a letter on his behalf is my expression of love towards him.

These are some of the positive forms of communication we shared. However, communication of negative feelings is as equally important in a marriage. My philosophy is "if you know then act" and I can only act based on what information I get. If hubby or I don't like something, we have the responsibility to inform each other. If the behavior persists, then it sends the message that the information was not received correctly or it was dismissed. If the latter is the case, then we make it a point to air it out. Experience has taught me that it is better to bring up personal gripes when your spouse is in a position to receive and respond to them positively and calmly. Only the two of you can decide when that is. My experience is that two minutes after walking in the door after a stressful day's work is not the best time for us. Perhaps, after making love may be a good time, or after a hearty meal and relaxing over a good movie or perhaps while taking a nice leisurely drive or gardening. To get the best results, remember that proper timing is everything. When you show your spouse that you respect his or her peace of mind, he or she would most likely receive even negative information positively. Your approach is very important; if you start offensively then your spouse will automatically put up the defenses, it's human nature. However, if you start with "Remember the other day when I said (fill in the blank) I think you didn't understand what I meant. What I meant was whenever (fill in the blank) is done it makes me feel (fill in the blank)." You fill in the blanks with your objective being getting your spouse to empathize with how an action or inaction has negatively affected you. You may even want to share if this action has a history from childhood or a prior negative experience that you haven't been quite able to move past as yet. Inviting your spouse into your psyche will put you in a vulnerable position however, the benefit of an understanding and empathetic mate in my opinion far outweigh the risks.

Hubby and I building on our innate way of expressing our love through communicating began to shape how we judge or prejudge each other's actions. For example, if he bought me a beautiful Pandora bracelet, I must understand that even though those funds could have gone on a much needed bill, I must appreciate that he is saying "I love you and I will figure out another way to make up for that bill." By me doing the laundry, putting up his clothes and hanging up his shirts in the closet my expression conveys "I love you and I know you work long hours so I am making things a little less laborious for you at home." My friends we must begin to mull through how our mates respond when we do and say things. It would be beneficial for you to purchase the Gary Chapman's, "The Five Love Languages," book and workbook and work through them as a couple. Understanding how you communicate, how you show and like to receive love will greatly benefit you in your relationship and I dear say help you to avoid many misunderstandings in how you communicate to one another verbally and especially non-verbally.

Hubby and I determined to use this great gift of communication to accentuate and build on our rich life together. This rich life is filled with talking with each other throughout the day, sharing jokes, frustrations of work, family, associates and each other frankly, or talking about the news of the day or me getting "on his case" about something or another he neglected. The joy of watching Ava grow, develop and communicate, or him sharing his day at work, or me complaining over how often his work phone rings when he's at home; like us discussing school options and social activities for Ava, guessing what she will be like as she grows older, taking weekend drives, and going on outings together. Whatever the topic, significant or not, we communicate about it.

COUPLE DISCUSSION AND APPLICATION SECTION:

Take out a notepad and write out your responses, then discuss openly and honestly with your spouse, fiancée or significant other.

1. What things do you do or say that express and communicate your love to your spouse?

2. How do you respond to your spouse when you are angry?

3. What things do you do to convey that you love your spouse on a daily basis?

4. How do you convey your anger and frustration to your spouse?

5. Do you feel threatened or uncomfortable when your spouse communicates anger?

6. List in order of priority, how you feel loved from your spouse. The order of the list will give you some insight as to how your spouse expresses love and wants to receive love.

When your spouse physically touches you _____
When your spouse puts your needs above the needs of self /others _____
When your spouse says positive words to you _____
When your spouse surprises you with gifts _____
When your spouse does things for you without you having to ask _____
When your spouse puts interests in your likes or recreation _____
When your spouse spends time with you and appears to enjoy doing so _____

PRINCIPLE #5

~

Continue to Date

Let's be honest folks, when we say "I do" we expect to spend the rest of our lives together. This practice of continued dating did not present as a challenge for hubby and me until we became parents. Therefore, our advice is that when you become parents, you must be careful not to become so emotionally involved with your children that you become detached from your spouses romantically. It is vital, even crucial, to find time to date with no kids and no friends around, even if it resorts to a lunch-time date.

Side bar to wives and moms and those of you planning to become mothers. Yes I'm talking to you new mothers and not so new mothers, those sweet babies when they come can consume our lives if we let them. They demand so much attention and by the time you're able to shift attention to your hubby, it's 10:30 p.m. and you're tired, worn out with seemingly nothing left to give. Now moms, this suggest it's time to be creative with your romantic and sex lives because experience has taught me that those little people can snuff out our sex pheromones better than a blood hound on a wounded fox. Trust me, I know they can throw a monkey wrench in spoiling the romantic mood. It's imperative that you take a few minutes out of your hectic baby and children schedule and give hubby some time. First of all: Lovemaking. This element of intimacy is crucial to satisfying your husband's physical desires and yours. Secondly, find time to go out with him without the children, whether it may be lunch on the beach, or sitting in a park, at your favourite spot or your favourite restaurant. Even those rare occasions can become a staple binding a lifetime connection for you both.

Side bar to husbands and fathers! The truth is, in order to get your wives to the place where she can even garner her thoughts around accommodating you sexually or otherwise, a few things ought to be in place to clear out some of the clutter in her hectic life. I wish to suggest that with a concerted team effort you both can build and sustain a romantic life in the midst of taxing home life. Husbands, you can go a long way in assisting in this effort by helping your wife around the house more, feeding the kids, bathing them, helping out with homework or playing with them while mom is in the kitchen. Also, helping out with the laundry or doing a chore without having being asked can go a long way. Another tip to you husbands out there with young families is assisting with domestic chores can go a long way into tapping into your wives soft side. There is nothing sexier to me than my hubby taking the initiative to do the laundry or watching him sit by the bathtub getting splashed by Ava while I take a break or attend to something else without having to worry getting her settled for bedtime. So husbands, in addition to lightening her load you're in turn lightening her mood which makes her less tired, more relaxed and makes you more sexually desirable. So even though she may be tired, instead of her settling in at 10:30 p.m. she may be able to go to bed at 9:30 p.m. giving you one full hour to romance her.

Some persons may be thinking, "My idea of dating is getting out of the house with no kids around" and yes that is the ideal. However, some seasons in your lives may rarely allow for that kind of experience, but, in the meantime, you must work with what time you have alone. In our marriage, there are seasons that hubby has to work projects for weeks at a time whereby he can't spend full weekends with us and during the weekdays he works so late Ava doesn't get to see him until the morning when he does daycare drop off.

But even then, he still tries to put in the time by calling me throughout the day and night to keep in touch with us. Even in those seasons, if he had to make a quick run he would call and say "I'm passing your work let's go pick up a quick snack or can you go with me on this quick run?" Though it was only an hour, that time was well spent because it expressed his sentiments "I want to take any opportunity to steal away a moment with you" and to me that sentiment is "priceless."

I don't know about your youthful experiences, but at age 13 -17 years old, I had an active social life whereby my parents were important but my friends were essential. So by the time your children become teenagers, either you and your spouse will be left to lick your wounds with your hands in the air trying to figure out "where to go from here." Or you will be happy dropping them off to the movies, so you and your spouse can finally tear up the house making love or finally being able to watch that movie that caught your attention during its trailer presentation.

Hubby and I enjoy going to the movies and eating those supersize candies which we don't normally get a chance to eat, then there are times we go to the "Fish Fry" which is local hot spot in The Bahamas where we live and we eat well seasoned fresh fried fish or grilled seafood as well as other local delicacies. Therefore, if we continue with these type of activities, whenever Ava moves into her teenage and adult life years, it will only free us up to spend even more time doing the things we were limited in when she was younger and required more parenting time.

My mom or "gammy" as Ava affectionately calls her is a homebody and so she and Ava have a great time together while we date. Advice to new parents! "Get close to your teenage cousins, friends, or single home-body friends if you don't have parents or other baby-sitters." Do your private vetting i.e. have them come over about an hour in advance to get a feel for their rapport with your children so you can vet the interaction and cancel if you sense any negative vibes. Also plan way in advance, as single persons often have busy lives, so ensure to call a week or two before your date night and follow-up a few days before the date. Also parents keep in mind the birthdates and favourite deserts and meals of your perspective baby-sitters so you will have less opposition when calling upon them or bribing their services. If not, get more creative and partner with other trust worthy married families who share your family values. You can plan to alternate once per month to keep the kids while you go dating.

When I was about fifteen years old or so, the guy I liked at the time would call me every Saturday morning and I learnt that his parents would go to a nice restaurant for breakfast every Saturday morning. About two years into my marriage, I went to a mid-day function at one of our local hotels and I was delighted to see his parents walking out of the hotel, no doubt coming from their scheduled Saturday breakfast after about fifty years of marriage. Did I mention that when we dated he was the youngest of six children? So don't use your children as an excuse. Children need stable, happy parents so by enriching your marriage life, you will be paying your children the biggest legacy of stability and how to measure true love and commitment.

You have only eighteen years to lay as many foundational blocks of life for them to build on. Therefore, building a successful marriage and family life can be critical to your children's emotional stability and success as adults. I challenge you to show affection to your spouse in the front of your children. I guarantee you will get their attention. If they're younger, like Ava, they will either stare, smile or try to break it up and if they are older they will likely make some snide gesture or remark. The point is either way you get their attention and whether they admit it or not it makes them feel more secure, knowing that in the midst of all the hardship they are exposed to in the world that at home, there is a place of safety and genuine love. The odds are they would seek to harness that same atmosphere of love and stability in their family lives and aspire to make their homes one where their children would feel they are loved, safe and secure.

The main idea is whether you're creative or traditional in your approach to dating, set that alone time together. Whether the date is thirty minutes or three hours just do it. Don't let the "singles" give you a reason to think you're missing out on some exciting, spectacular experience. Whatever activities, social events or outings you enjoyed while dating, take time to enjoy them every so often. Your regular time may be weekly, bi-weekly or monthly *just do it regularly* and as much as humanly possible and do not allow anyone or anything besides sickness, or death to alter your love life.

COUPLE DISCUSSION AND APPLICATION SECTION:

Take out a notepad and write out your responses, then discuss openly and honestly with your spouse, fiancée or significant other.

1. List all of the things you and your spouse did while dating.

2. Do you still do any of those things today? If not, why not?

3. Do you have a regular date night? If not, why not?

4. If you haven't already discussed setting a regular date night or dating time, do so.

PRINCIPLE #6

~

Don't Sweat The Small Stuff

One of the most valuable pieces of marriage advice that I remember, hold dear and share with every young lady at her wedding shower is "Don't sweat the small stuff." This advice came from a colleague of mine who had been married over twenty five years. She told me during my pre-marriage advice sharing time "don't bother arguing over the toothpaste cap being left open or the toilet seat being left up, if it's open close it, if it's up just put it down, he had to put the seat up after you used it, just don't sweat it." This short fifteen second piece of advice resonated with me tremendously, because I was getting advice from many places and was warned about how horrifying the first year, first five years and first seven years would be.

Fortunately, some very close girlfriends had already been married a few years prior to me and they offered a good support system whenever I had to share an issue I had with my husband and thought no one else on the planet would understand. In essence, they would be able to complete my story or gripe, so I quickly learned that hubby and I weren't special or exempt, conflict was a right of passage in a marriage. Because there are so many firsts in a marriage, bumps in the road were unavoidable.

On the day I wrote this chapter, I had a conversation with a friend who lost her husband of twenty-two years after his two-year battle with prostate cancer. He left a wife and three daughters. I was so shaken after learning of his death. I couldn't imagine what she was going through, the first night sleeping in a bed she knew he would never embrace her in again, or kiss his girls again and walk them down the aisle. Then I reflected on my number one marriage advice, not to sweat the small stuff. What would my friend give to have her husband leave the toilet seat up or have him forget to take out the trash or snore so hard it woke her out of her sleep? What would she give for just one more night? This death had really put things into perspective for me.

About seven months after we were married hubby and I attended a marriage conference and the facilitators in one of the sessions invited all the couples to do an exercise with them. They had the lights turned off, and asked the wives to place their heads on their husbands' shoulders. They narrated us walking through the funeral scene of our spouses. The scenario began with the surviving spouse coming in through the funeral hallways, walking closer and closer toward the coffin and then being up close and seeing him or her for the last time. We were instructed to say what was on our hearts, share our regrets, our joys, what he or she meant to us, how much he or she would be missed. Then we had to imagine being seated and watching our spouse's image fade as the body was being lowered into the coffin and the lid was being slowly closed signaling the last time we would see his or her physical image again. Needless to say, when the lights turned on, the room was flooded with teary eyed wives and red-eyed husbands. It was the first time hubby and I ever had to confront life without each other in it. It was probably advantageous to us that we were exposed to that kind of sensitivity training early on in our marriage. We were forced to imagine what would be going on in our hearts and on our minds during such a horrendous experience.

For us, we shared our regrets of not being able to start a family together and raise kids and not saying we loved each other enough. This was an awakening moment. Here again, my number one marriage advice resounded with me. During those moments, very little seemed matter to us, just those things that enhanced our relationship mattered and the days following as we reflected on that experience.

Folks, I admonish you, don't sweat the small stuff in your marriage, it's not your parents' home anymore, you get to make the rules together. Yes, there are some things that really get under your skin but the truth is, it's your issue not your spouse's issue. You can only change you! However, if you make the right decision in choosing a mate who value your feelings, with sensible discussion your mate should appreciate your pet peeves and make an effort to meet you half way.

One of my pet-peeves is leaving a cup or a plate in the sink after all the dishes have been cleaned, especially overnight. For me, when hubby does that I perceive the message that he doesn't care about my efforts. But the reality is he had a housekeeper in his parents' home for much of his life and when he was off to college he utilized the dishwasher, so he's was not being vindictive, just lazy and spoilt. Therefore, I had to deal with my own feelings and practice not transferring them to him. Most times, I let it go and when I don't he would sense my sharp stare and would smile and go wash the dirty dish as my eyes led him to the point of his miss-step. Even if he didn't, I had to be fair, he was spoilt when it came to domestic issues, but he would do the laundry without my bidding, mow the lawn or pay someone to do it, take out the garbage, change the water filter, change all the light bulbs, make home repairs and the list goes on. He would do all those things that aren't everyday jobs, but equally as important and ones that I quite frankly don't do, don't attempt to do and don't care to do, so I call us even.

The bottom line is be fair, list the things that your spouse assumes without your assistance and you will likely see how much value they have in the marriage and family life, much of it that goes unnoticed or isn't bragged about. Just don't sweat the small stuff.

COUPLE DISCUSSION AND APPLICATION SECTION:

Take out a notepad and write out your responses, then discuss openly and honestly with your spouse, fiancée or significant other.

1. List five (5) things your spouse, fiancée or significant other does to make your life easier or more comfortable.

2. What financial/monetary value would you place on the chores your spouse does in the home and within the marriage?

3. What things do you complain about your spouse, fiancée or significant other that you can personally change or influence?

4. What things do you complain about your spouse, fiancée or significant other that you cannot change or influence?

5. What are some of your pet-peeves regarding your spouse, fiancée or significant other?

6. What can he/she do to minimize or avoid offending you in these pet-peeves?

PRINCIPLE #7
~
Create Your Own Paradise

Hubby and I went to a wedding about a year after we got married and the officiator's charge to the bride and groom was to *"create their own paradise."* He continued on to iterate saying to them that, "If you could only afford corn beef, eat it under the candle light and if you could only afford Kool-Aid then drink it in your wine glass or plastic cup and enjoy your paradise. If your neighbour asked what you had for dinner, respond by stating you had "beef and punch." The congregation roared with laughter, but his words and the implication behind them were serious. As I sat there, I pondered this simple advice because it resonated so powerfully with me.

So often people of all walks of life become stressed, depressed, oppressed and in debt because they may be living up to some external standard of what society; family, friends or foe, think their lives should reflect. In this hopeless pursuit of happiness, they may question why they find themselves feeling empty and unfulfilled.

First of all, in your paradise you must be able to understand the difference between roles and chores. A role is a duty that you should perform such as a husband providing leadership and protection for his spouse and children or the wife's role to support her husband as they chart the course for their family unit.

A chore is an action that has no gender specific role such as cleaning, cooking, gardening, etc. So many times couples become confused with those two concepts and allow the outside world to box them into chores adopting them as roles causing undo stress and conflict within a marriage.

I also wish to interject that as a female, I came to respect and embrace my husband's role in our marriage as the leader and protector instead of becoming offended by or adopting the perception of him "ruling" over me. The truth is that in any society or organization that is deemed successful, there exists a hierarchy or a head that is responsible or accountable for the success of that organization. Therefore, we operate our marriage under this premise with me as the deputy head who shares in the decision making and planning of the family unit, just as the board of directors partner toward the success of an organization.

Secondly, when I consider the concept of a paradise, I think of a sort of oasis or place of tranquility and peace of mind and I am led to reflect on what position we will be in during the end of our lives. I question what will matter most to us? What will we be saying to each other in those final moments? What will we be regretting in those moments and thereafter? Will it be, instead of the BMW, we should have bought the Corolla, then we would have been able to afford Ava's last year of college? Or will it be, although we didn't get the two-storey house with the pool and the expensive car in the driveway, we were able to attend most of Ava's recitals, extracurricular activities and afford sending her to college. We took family vacations or traveled around the world. We can now enjoy our wonderful children and grandchildren with fulfilling careers and rich family and community life. The decisions and plans we make will be a reflection of how we defined our paradise inclusive of priorities, recreation, finances, time and resources among other things.

The choice is yours. Before marriage, you should create a mental and physical blueprint of your individual, marital and family goals. This blueprint can range from career and professional development, travelling to Italy or Paris as a couple, saving for your children's college tuition or purchasing a piece of real estate for your children or starting a business venture together. Although you may not have done so, it is never too late to re-shape your existing structure. Do expect your plans to be altered in this winding road of life with car repairs, plumbing, electrical failures, dental repairs, taxes and unexpected medical bills. However, you can always get back on track and have few regrets for doing it the way you both agreed upon.

COUPLE DISCUSSION AND APPLICATION SECTION:

Take out a notepad and write out your responses, then discuss openly and honestly with your spouse, fiancée or significant other.

1. What is your ideal paradise? Describe it: home, car, job, family life, recreation, retirement, etc.

2. List in order of priority, each description in your paradise.

3. How can you merge your lists of priority to benefit your personal and relationship goals?

4. List up to 5 personal successes or achievements?

5. How have your personal successes benefitted your relationship?

6. List up to 5 successes and achievements as a couple.

7. How has your collaborated successes/achievements benefitted your relationship?

8. What do you believe the role of a husband and wife is? Does your marriage or relationship reflect that belief?

PRINCIPLE #8

~

Safeguards

After discussing my manuscript with a few colleagues who were married within the past five years, I was asked to add a few comments on safeguards. Life is filled with safeguards that we take for granted. Safeguards are things put in place to protect us from danger, like traffic lights to limit accidents, stair railings to limit falls and bed railings for babies to limit a head or bodily injury. Just as smoke detectors serve to caution us of impending dangers, safeguards in one's marriage should serve as caution of impending conflict if certain boundaries are crossed. These boundaries should be predicated on mutual respect and accountability.

Sometimes men and women's egos may get in the way, seeking to hold on to what is considered "autonomy and personal control." They may fight against someone telling them how and what they should or shouldn't do. It's human nature to "kick against the pricks," similar to kids when they attempt to sneak a cookie out of the cookie jar after being warned not to do so. Spouses sometimes are challenged in how they view giving and getting respect and being accountable for their behaviors, whereabouts, finances and future.

However, the rules of engagement for a successful and prosperous marriage require safeguards to protect the life of the marriage and the hearts and peace of minds of our spouses that will stand the tests of time. Hubby and I practice at least four safeguards that have helped us to maintain mutual respect and accountability for and toward each other.

I. Safeguard your past and present behaviors:

Everyone has a history whether boring or highly decorated. Contrary to popular slogans and opinions from grandmas that, "it is best not to let all the dirty linen out of the closet before you get married," we have often discovered that the world gets smaller every day. So, if you shared an act or relationship with someone else, then it's no longer a secret, and you no longer have control over its keeping. The open door honesty policy safeguards future spousal blindsiding that can have great repercussions and even lead to the demise of your union. If trust is broken, it is hard to rebuild. When hubby and I dated we seemingly talked about everything; past relationships, failures and shortcomings. As the relationship progressed, we evolved to being accountable for our whereabouts, not as a control mechanism, but as a method of staying connected with each other throughout the day. This practice continues in our marriage today. However, a month or two before the wedding, a friend whispered to me that she heard my fiancée may have cheated on me, and she gave a scenario involving another person. After listening to her I just laughed silently to myself. I did this because my fiancée had already shared the nature of his relationship with this person, and I was personally settled that he was being truthful. If he didn't volunteer this information with me prior to me hearing the news from someone else, this could have been detrimental to our relationship. I later learned that the original talebearers had disingenuous motives. The importance of this safeguard is to shield your marriage from others with alternative motives.

II. Safeguard and be accountable for your whereabouts:

I remember as a pre-teen when my uncle visited our home, before he left, he told my grandaunt that he was leaving. My mom and I came home shortly there after. It was not long before we all heard a big crash, which urged my grandaunt to have us go out to the main road to see what had happened because she knew my uncle had just left us. To our dismay, it was his car that got into an accident. I know this may seem old fashioned, especially in modern times where many persons live on their own from early adulthood. However, at a young age I learned that accountability in families has its place and especially now in a marriage it is equally as important. Fortunately my uncle wasn't badly injured but what if he was and we weren't aware of his whereabouts?

Hubby and I both work in environments where we have female and male colleagues who also are friends. If he goes out to lunch and a female colleague wanted to tag along, he would, call me and jokingly say "I have my sweetheart out with me, I'm just letting you know in case someone calls to gossip." I would do the same, but now we have built such a strong level of trust and security in our relationship we don't have to do that as often but still do it out of respect and as a safeguard we either call or mention it later on as we recap events of our day.

Whenever hubby is working late, he would call to say that he is on his way and we would usually talk until he arrives. This practice allows me to gauge his safety on his way home. I, too, would call when Ava and I arrive home to follow-up on his day or to report Ava's deeds of the day. This practice gives us both peace of mind and keeps us connected to each other all day even though we don't speak every minute.

Many times family, friends or colleagues would mention that they saw one of us somewhere and almost immediately we would be able to identify where or what each other was up to. Therefore, I dare say, I would be the first to come to hubby's defense if his reputation was questioned because he was placed somewhere or another that is uncharacteristic of his typical whereabouts. In a marriage, it is crucial that couples feel secure and that each spouse can be trusted to be where he or she purports to be but also be secure that if there is a detour, that a viable explanation is not second guessed or questioned.

III. Safeguard your finances:

I can recall my grandmother stating in a comical tone

during a social event with friends that "what was hers was hers and what was his (referring to my grandfather) was hers." Though comical many women view their husband's finances as theirs but not vice versa.

Ladies, sorry to burst your bubbles, but that's not the proper concept. You must both pool your resources to enrich the family's resources. When I met my husband, I was making twice his salary. However, when he completed his degree within a few months, I lost my part-time employment and he got full employment which exceeded my salary placing him in better financial standing than me. However, I saved a lot when I had the additional income and these funds came in handy when we began building our home. The additional savings covered all of our banking, legal and closing fees.

Finances is a delicate topic I believe because initially when couples date they take for granted that their money is theirs, therefore they get to decide on how to spend it. This, in essence, is true because they are single. Also most men during the courting period tend to wine and dine the female per se, paying for the dinners, movie tickets and giving the gifts. It is not until marriage that the true financial dilemma surface when one spouse has to adjust to the other spouse's spending habits. This is the time when one spouse discovers that the other may be more spendthrift while he or she may not be that way. A man may seem to gamble with spending because he believes he can always make the money through overtime or other efforts, while the woman is concerned about maintaining the security of the family life. She may be the one who stresses about the bills being paid, leaving needs unmet and so on. Safeguarding finances entail spouses curtailing and managing their spending habits and deciding on what is priority versus luxury or in other words what is necessary now and what can wait until later. Unfortunately, financial discord if not tempered can also lead to the dysfunction or demise of a union.

Another aspect of financial safeguards is spouses recognizing the value of monetary and non-monetary contributions to the family life. Ladies, if you do most of the house work and he pays most of the bills don't try to measure or equate the value of each contribution! How can you measure either of those most necessary assets to your family development and quality of life? Gents, if your wife makes more money than you do but she has no worries when her car breaks down, the house fixtures fall apart, helping out with the household chores, who can estimate the value of your contribution to the quality of your family life. I will reiterate to my readers please don't count, try to measure or equate the value of each contribution you make, you will always fall short. This is a very important point because it reconnects us to the principle of being unified in all that we possess, enabling us to move closer into solidifying the "oneness" that marriage should typify. My youth leader was once asked why he and his wife shared a bank account and he responded "If I could trust my wife with my most sacred possession *"my heart"* why shouldn't I trust her with my money." This statement should be the mantra in our approach to how we view our finances as a couple. "What is his is ours and what is hers is ours."

IV. Safeguard your future:

Benjamin Franklin said, "There are only two things certain in life: death and taxes." He was a wise man. In marriage, we tend to focus on living our best life and growing our families to be productive members of the society.

We rarely think about what life would be like without our spouses in it. We should, even though it is such an emotional and dreadful thought. We must face it head on and be prepared, or at least ensure our spouses and children have the security of knowing their quality of life does not end with our demise. Besides love and fond memories, there should be a legacy of financial security. Let's think about it. Earlier, I shared with you about a friend who lost her husband. When I spoke to her, she shared that the mortgage was covered because of her bank's policy of mandatory life insurance coverage in the amount of the mortgage. However, she was still plagued with an eighty thousand dollar debt because of her husband's medical bills and decrease in the family's income when he became ill and had to leave work. This type of situation is so tragic but so typical of married couples as we become so engrossed in living in the present that we forget about the future, especially dying. Therefore, as a couple if you haven't put in place financial safeguards in the event of the demise of your spouse you should seriously make an effort to begin doing so. You can use methods such as, investments like stock, bonds, and the like or life insurance policies, saving plans etc. You should begin to assess which method best suits the present and future fiscal and budgetary constraints of your growing family and get going.

COUPLE DISCUSSION AND APPLICATION SECTION:

Take out a notepad and write out your responses, then discuss openly and honestly with your spouse, fiancée or significant other.

Accountability for past and present behaviors.

1. List some of the most shameful behaviors you committed in your past, e.g. cheating on a previous girlfriend/boyfriend.

2. Was your spouse aware of those behaviors prior to this discussion? If not, why not?

3. Do you share your mistakes and short-comings with your spouse? For example, feelings of insecurity when spouse is in the company of the opposite gender?

Accountability for Whereabouts

1. Does your spouse know the route you take to and from work?

2. Does your spouse know the approximate times you get off from work?

3. When you leave the house, does your spouse know when and where you are going?

4. Does your spouse have to call to ask when you will be coming home more often than not? Or do you take the initiative to inform him or her before being asked?

Accountability for Finances

1. Do you know your spouse's total income? If not do you feel comfortable sharing your financial status with your spouse? If not, why?

2. If you receive a bonus or additional income, would you tell your spouse? If not, why not?

3. Would you take your last $100 to meet the need of your spouse? If not, why not?

4. What was your parents' practice on sharing financial information with each other?

5. What can you do to feel more comfortable in sharing your finances with your spouse?

6. Do you think your family life will be better or worse by merging your finances to meet a family goal e.g. a home, repair, a family vacation etc.? Why?

Accountability for the future

1. In the event of your untimely demise would your family have any financial resources to cover the mortgage and other major loans? If not, why not?

2. How will your family be able to manage financially without your income?

3. How much do you think your spouse and children could survive on if you died today?

4. Will your present financial status, e.g. savings, cause your family to have less financial struggle in your absence?

5. Do you have a life insurance policy or other financial investments? If not, why not?

6. What measures can you put in place to ensure the financial security of your spouse and children in the event of your death?

If most of your responses are in the negative then list and discuss what things you can do to become more accountable to each other on a daily basis and safeguard your future. Also, a financial advisor may be beneficial in guiding you through your financial planning process.

PRINCIPLE #9

~

Divorce is Not an Option

When hubby and I decided to get married we resolved that for us divorce was not an option. Before I discuss why we made this resolve, I must interject that we both acknowledge that not every couple's marriage will stand the test of time. If someone is in an abusive or adulterous relationship whereby the spouse is unwilling to seek help and change, we do not advocate anyone continue to subject himself or herself to that marriage. However, we personally believe that too many people get divorced for frivolous reasons under the guise of "irreconcilable differences." Our thoughts on this principle are concise and simple. If divorce is not an option then we have to find a workable solution for our fork in the road and find a way to move past it. After we say our disagreement or issue is over, we must mean it and live and act accordingly.

Our first major argument came about three months into our marriage, I was so furious I went to my mom to spend the night. She didn't question me much, she only asked if we had a disagreement and if I was fine. The next morning she informed me that I made my choice and had to live with it and in her gentle way advised that her home is not a refuge for my marriage, my husband was. Wow! I thought! "This from a woman who has never been married." Needless to say that day and the next few days hubby and I were in survival communication mode until things went back to normal. I can honestly say to this day I can't even remember what we argued about so now I see how silly I was for staying away from my husband over something that really wasn't that serious. The next major blow out came up about three months later on Mother's Day, when he decided to take his mom to lunch at his workplace at the hotel. Now before you begin to judge me, I love my mother in law and my gripe wasn't about her personally. You see, since my husband began working at the hotel, I begged him countless times to take me there for dinner. His response would be "I don't like the people (i.e. his coworkers) to know my business" "I go to work almost everyday, I don't want to go there for dinner, and have people making remarks or asking me about work issues." Of course I thought it was a poor defense but, since he was so adamant about it, I grew to accept his stance.

Therefore, all the fires of hell began to burn within me when he told me that he was taking his mom for brunch at the hotel. Besides being angry, I was hurt and felt second class to his mother. Even though our parents are our first loves, I was of the opinion that when one married, it meant that parents came after the spouse and children. Well, I refused to let it go, I didn't go to my mom but I gave the infamous silent treatment, I slept into the front room of the apartment for a bit and to my dismay, my loving husband was somewhat unapologetic which made me even more furious. So I decided to call out the big gun, my father-in-law, who hubby respected deeply. Also, at that juncture I began to bond with him so wonderfully because he voluntarily adopted the role as my surrogate father, since my dad died when I was 17. Dad, as I affectionately call him is a precious man, who I have grown to love dearly. Dad mediated our venting session and in his peaceable fashion, tried to take on the blame for his son's actions.

Well, we aired out our feelings and after dad left, we decided that we couldn't allow our marriage to cause us to not communicate because that was the lifeblood of our relationship. We both admitted that the past week was the most miserable we both had in a long time and we vowed not to put ourselves through it again. Since then, whenever we disagree about something, we air our feelings, argumentatively, passionately, reasonably, unreasonably and then move on. Oh by the way, I have enjoyed several wonderful hotel dinners since that time.

Fortunately for us, we had good examples of how to survive the tests within marriages without even realizing it. My in-laws, my dad and step-mom were our models as they operated their relationships generally in the same way we do. I spent most weekends and holidays with my father and step-mom and was exposed to married life. My dad overcame his drug addiction very early on in his marriage. He went on to enjoy his and my step-mom's three children. I and another half-brother spent most weekends with them until our dad's demise and even thereafter. I observed that they would, at times, have the most heated arguments. Strangers looking in may have thought blows were on the precipice but literally within fifteen to thirty minutes they would be calm. My dad would come in and ask my step-mom to make him a sandwich or come into the room with a calm voice, sharing that he was going out and ask if she needed him to bring her anything back. At first this was surprising to me, but afterward this became like second nature.

Now that I think about it, I can be like that. At times I get hot-headed about an issue and then after I dispel the heat, it's over for me. Going back to my dad and step-mom, I think even more so after his victory over his drug addiction, they both resolved that they were in it for the long haul or like the vows recited on their wedding day stated "until death did them part." So I can safely say that six months into the marriage, my husband and I affirmed also that we were in it for the long haul, come hell or high water and whatever that entailed.

My in-laws have been married over forty years to date and I have enjoyed watching them laugh together and back-talk each other while I or hubby try to quietly referee their humorous banters they think are arguments. With real life and authentic models like them, hubby and I have great expectations of enjoying a long prosperous marriage.

COUPLE DISCUSSION AND APPLICATION SECTION:

Take out a notepad and write out your responses, then discuss openly and honestly with your spouse, fiancée or significant other.

1. Why did I get married?

   a. For what purpose?
   b. To achieve what end?

2. What could my spouse do that I could never forgive him or her and why?

3. Would can I do that my spouse would never forgive me for?

4. Have I made the conscious decision to stick with my marriage for the long haul?

5. Is divorce an option for me and if so under what circumstance would I consider it?

PRINCIPLE #10

~

Ourness

I attended a seminar in 2011 and one of the presenters talked about the importance of moving from the concept of "mine to ours" in solidifying a marriage. This sense of "ourness" suggests a sense of oneness that transcends self-promotion and a sense of personal denial for the betterment of the relationship. This concept encapsulated the idea that if a decision, act or behavior isn't beneficial to "us" or "our" well being as a family unit, then it isn't beneficial at all.

As I contemplated on these sentiments I realized that marriage calls for spouses to open themselves to the epitome of self-less-ness, that is, for myself and hubby to deny our own wills for the sake of our marriage. That's some heavy stuff! Then I realized that I was being hypocritical in my ambivalence to adapt this principle to my marital relationship even though I have practiced it in a multiplicity of other relationships. If you are honest with yourselves, so have you.

If you're a dedicated parent, you most definitely practice the essence of this concept. If you work for an external employer and give ideas and services to benefit the company or worked a few hours overtime or worked your lunchtime all with no compensation, you've demonstrated the ability to work on the "ourness" principle. If you've denied yourself a pair of shoes, that appliance or jewellery you've wanted or vacation to save for your child's college fund or to reward him or her for a good school report card then you have demonstrated the ability to work the "ourness" principle. If you've ever went to a dinner, recital or outing with your parent, sibling or best friend just to support them even though you would have much rather been at home in bed or elsewhere, you have demonstrated the ability to work the "ourness" principle.

You see, we've put our desires, our well-being, our time and the like on the back burner so that someone else would be happy and for the greater good. This is what the principle of "ourness' simply requires. You must put the enhancement and enrichment of your marriage before your own personal short-term happiness so that you both can reap the long term reward of unity, respect, trust, peace of mind and loyalty that will far outweigh that fleeting, temporal good feel of your own personal endeavours.

Typically men and women have different tastes in their preferences, ranging from food, recreation and friends. This doesn't mean that they may not share many commonalities. For example, both hubby and I love to go to the movies and we both love McDonalds. However, he loves to watch reality shows and I am more of a comedy and drama kind of girl. After the entrance of Miss Ava into our lives, we don't get to frequent the movies as much as we use to, so we opt to watch cable or order a movie. Since we both enjoy watching television, I have come to enjoy watching reality shows with a crime or nature element. He, on the other hand, has become a fan of legal, detective and comedy centric shows. Due to our little person, we have both been subjected from time to time to become fans of toddler shows. In all seriousness, in those times we spend watching television, we talk, laugh and learn about each other's viewpoints about the shows and life in general.

That was a lighthearted illustration, but a marriage brings forth a plethora of simple and complex dilemmas. For example, deciding on the purchase of a new car for hubby because his air conditioner is busted and the nine year old car's wear and tear has taken its toll but also recognizing that if hubby could hold on for another year or two, that small credit card loan would be paid off freeing funds for the new car loan, providing less of a financial burden on the family budget.

Perhaps the wife likes having her manicures, pedicures and hair done twice per month. Although, it is vitally important to look attractive, that additional hundred dollars may be better utilized if added to the mortgage monthly. This can reduce the loan principle, freeing the family to full home ownership rights in 20 years instead of 25 years. This would allow more financial freedom during the children's college years. Therefore, mom reducing her bi-monthly salon appointments to once per month would benefit the family in the long-term. Simple things like consulting each other before making little or big plans, putting your own desires aside for the benefit and happiness of your spouse and the success of your family life expresses your maturity and determination to set your marriage on the road to great success and prosperity. These all solidify the transition from the concept of "mine" to "ours," which sets the foundation for a more unified relationship and marital bond because you now realize that if your spouse is lacking then so are you but, in turn, if your spouse is prospering you too shall also reap the benefits.

COUPLE DISCUSSION AND APPLICATION SECTION:

Take out a notepad and write out your responses, then discuss openly and honestly with your spouse, fiancée or significant other.

1. What have you ever deprived yourself of that benefitted your spouse?

2. What have you ever deprived yourself of that benefitted your family life?

3. Do you believe a married couple should share financial assets e.g. a bank account? If so, why? and if not, why not?

4. What practical changes can you make in your personal life to create an atmosphere of "ourness" in your relationship?

5. How can you merge the following things to enhance the spirit of oneness in your relationship?

   a. Financially
   b. Recreationally
   c. Socially
   d. Spiritually

FINAL WORD

When hubby and I decided to get married we had enjoyed lives filled with travelling the world, socializing, educating ourselves and the like so marriage was our next bold step. As I pen these final words I am pondering where those first five years have gone? It seemed like yesterday. I remembered my limousine turning into the church yard and I saw this fine specimen of a gentlemen coming out of his limousine decked in his pure white suit and dark sun glasses. For the first time in the four months of wedding planning, I allowed myself to get excited, and I remembered feeling emotional. It was my confirmation that this decision was the right one, and there was no looking back for me.

Perhaps you're still working on your academic or professional dreams, you may already have children, don't have your dream job yet, but that's okay. It's perfectly okay to go into the marriage with personal goals left undone. The important thing is that your spouse, fiancé or significant other respects your dreams and realizes that when you are all that you can be, then it only makes for a more successful, enriched marriage. Unity says, "I know you and understand you and we will work it all out together as we go along day by day." Wherever the station in your married life and relationship, know that there is much hope for success if you would sit back, review and revise where you are going and how to get there. I hope that applying these principles will reinforce your marriage commitment and success. Also, that your discussions will aid you in setting the foundation necessary to reaching your life goals together as you seek to survive all the tests life will throw at you as a couple.

In life, people rarely remember how you began the race, but they often remember how you complete the race. This suggests that the path between the two offers much hope to gain ground toward a successful end. You may have begun your marriage journey on a rocky road by reality setting in on the trip to your honeymoon through missing your flight and having your first blame-game argument, or you threatening to go back to your parents after a hurtful word or deed was done. However, if you both resolve in your hearts that there are no refunds and no returns and you try to implement and fine tune these principles within the confines of your relationship, you are bound for a lifetime of success, happiness and true contentment in your relationship. I wish you much blessings and adventure as you live, love and laugh a lifetime away together as you pass your tests of difficult times during your marriage journey!

DEDICATION

Forever I Do, is dedicated to my loving husband Giles, my inspiration, best friend, confidante and cheerleader and also to our beautiful and vivacious daughter Ava.

REFERENCES

Principle 2

"Genesis 2:24 (King James New Version)." In Bible Gateway. Accessed January 19, 2014. http://www.biblegateway.com/passage/?search=GENESIS+2&version=CJB.

Principle 4

Chapman, G. D. (1992, 1993) The Five Love Languages, Chicago, IL: (Northfield Publishing).

Principle 9

Benjamin Franklin, in a letter to Jean-Baptiste Leroy, 1789, "Our new Constitution is now established, and has an appearance that promises permanency; but in this world nothing can be said to be certain, except **death and taxes**." http://en.wikipedia.org/wiki/Death_&_Taxes